Jean and
25.12.1990

Alan and

ERNST HAUSNER · VIENNA

ERNST HAUSNER
VIENNA
INTRODUCTION
AND
REMINISCENCE
EDITION WIEN

The author is responsible for preparing
texts and pictures, and for the design,
layout and technical production supervision.

Translation into English by Gertrude Maurer.

Typeset and made up for printing on IBM Personal Computer.

IBM

Desktop-Publishing Oliver Hausner.

Colour separation: Krammer Repro Druckformen GmbH, Linz
Printers: Edelbacher Druck Ges.m.b.H., Wien
Book binders: Gerald Frauenberger, Neudörfl
Typeface: 8/9/10 pt Bodoni
Paper: 150 g Magnostar of Leykam-Mürztaler
Papier- und Zellstoff-AG, Gratkorn.

ISBN 3-85058-001-6

Printed in Austria.
This book has also been published in Chinese, French,
German, Italian, Japanese and Russian.

Sixth Edition, 1997.

Vienna is the capital of the Republic of Austria
and seat of the Nationalrat, Bundesrat,
Federal President, Federal Government,
the Administrative and Constitutional Court and
the highest federal administration bodies.

In addition to New York and Geneva,
Vienna is an official seat of the United Nations,
with the International Atomic Energy Agency (IAEA),
the United Nations Industrial Development Organisation (UNIDO)
and another 51 sub-organisations,
headquarters of the Organisation
of Petroleum Exporting Countries (OPEC),
and of the Conflict Prevention Centre
of the 52 CSCE member states.

"Vindobona" marked on a copy of a Roman road map, around 370. "Peutingeriana", Nationalbibliothek.

Ever since prehistoric times, the Vienna Basin, a down-fault nestling between Alps and Carpathians, has been settled by humans. It was there that the "Amber Street", the trading route that linked the Baltic and Adriatic Seas, came upon the East-West route along the Danube. The continuity of settlement that survived the centuries and a location excellently suited to dominate its surrounding favoured the development of the region.

When the Romans moved their frontiers across the Alps, incorporating the Celtic kingdom of Noricum (including the area around Vienna) in their province of Pannonia in 15 BC, Vienna first entered the stage of history. The Danube served as the commercial and administrative border of the Roman Empire. "Vindobona" was established as a military camp in 100 AD. A network of roads was built to foster traffic and commerce; the *municipium* of Vindobona, a Roman civilian town near an ancient Celtic settlement, grew to more than 15,000 inhabitants.

Around 400 AD, Vindobona was destroyed under the onslaught of Germanic tribes. Over the next century, the Romans withdrew from Pannonia, with the Germanic tribes following hard on their heels. Remains of the former military camp continued to be settled throughout the subsequent era of mass migration. In a steady battle with tribes from the East (Avars, Magyars, 955), the Carolingians from Bavaria succeeded in colonising the country and converting it to Christianity.

The Babenbergs, a colonising dynasty and margraves of the German Empire since 976, came to rule in Vienna around 1135, finally moving their court there in 1155 (and were elevated to dukes in 1156). Recorded in the annals of 1137 as a regular community boasting a market and judicial court(*civitas*), Vienna was a full-fledged urban centre already in the early 13th century, leader in trade and culture and one of the great cities on the north side of the Alps. Surrounded by a wall and moat, it extended to approximately the size of today's inner city.

When the last Babenberg (Frederick II) died in 1246, the duchy and city fell to King Premysl Ottocar II of Bohemia. It was under his stewardship that the Romanesque part of the Stephansdom and the oldest part of the Hofburg, the Schweizer Trakt, were built. In 1278, Ottocar II was felled battling King Rudolf I of Habsburg; as a consequence, "Austria below the Enns" and Vienna remained under Habsburg's rule for over 600 years.

The 14th century was a period of consolidation for the temporal powers, and it saw the growth of Gothic Vienna. The Gothic choir in the Stephansdom was completed. Duke Rudolf IV, in many ways the most remarkable and outstanding character of his time (*Privilegium maius)*, laid the foundation stone to the nave and tower of the cathedral (1359) and founded a university in 1365. The charter of 1396 granted equal status to artisans, traders and patricians - thereby warding off from Vienna the fate of other cities where sanguine fights had broken out over the issue.

Family squabbles within the Habsburgs, disputes with the citizenry of Vienna (execution of Mayor Vorlauf, in 1408, and Mayor Holzer, in 1463), political instability, an insecure grip of power on the part of Frederick III (1440 to 1493, Holy Roman

First record of "Wien" (last but one line, right-hand side). Salzburger Annalen, 881. Stiftsarchiv Admont.

Frederick III's charter granting a coat-of-arms to the City of Vienna, 1461. Section. Wiener Landesarchiv.

Emperor as of 1452), and an economic decline accompanied the 15th century. In 1485, Vienna capitulated to King Matthias Corvinus of Hungary, only to surrender to the Emperor again after the Hungarian's death.

In the 16th century, Central Europe was in the throes of Lutheran teaching, while its borders were simultaneously facing an ever more critical onslaught from the Turks. In 1522, the estates unsuccessfully rebelled against their souvereign (suppressed by the Court of Wiener Neustadt where Mayor Siebenbürger was decapitated); and in 1526, a new charter abolished almost all the rights formerly enjoyed by Vienna. In 1529, the Turks lay siege to Vienna, only to be defeated. Becoming Imperial Residence again in 1533, Vienna gained in its standing by the new absolutism (Ferdinand I) and the introduction of centralised administration (Bohemia and Hungary). The medieval wall was replaced by bastions and glacis, which remained in place until the 19th century. Suburbs and villages sprang up outside the glacis, dominated by trade and industry.

In the first half of the 17th century, fanatic religious strife (around 1575, four out of five Viennese were Protestants) brought victory to the Catholic Counter-Reformation (Jesuits, Cardinal Khlesl), which was supported by the Empire. Numerous orders were called to Vienna, and their churches, built in the early Baroque style, have placed an indelible mark on the cityscape. In 1679, a severe epidemic of the plague killed one third of the populace (a column commemorating the event was erected on the Graben).

View of Vienna from the south, panel painting around 1470. Master of the Schottenaltar, Schottenstift, Vienna.

Baroque Vienna. The Old Town. Section of Joseph Daniel Huber's bird's eye view, 1785.

In 1683, the Turks once again laid siege to Vienna. Their crushing defeat laid the ground for the creation of the Baroque imperial capital and residence where the newly empowered court and church, a aristocracy vastly enriched and society in general glorified their victories in a union of all branches of art and culture. The Imperial Library, Karlskirche, Peterskirche, Piaristenkirche, Schönbrunn, Belvedere, Prince Eugene of Savoy's winter palace, the palaces of the Schwarzenbergs, Trautsons, Schönborns, Harrachs and Kinskys, the aula of the Old University - they all were designed to celebrate in stone the spirit of the time. L.v. Hildebrandt and J.B. Fischer von Erlach, architects of great standing, built their masterpieces, music flourished thanks to masters such as Gluck, Haydn and Mozart. A second line of fortifications (Gürtel) was built to protect the suburbs, their palaces and summer residences.

Manufactories came into existence, marking the transition from trade to production. Maria Theresa (1740-1780) and Joseph II (1780-1790) introduced sweeping reforms in line with a modern absolutist state governed by civil servants, reforms which encompassed politics, administration, law and education. Vienna became the capital of a centralist state. Joseph II, in his enlightened centralism, captured contemporary concerns by promoting science, technology and educa- tion, equality before the law, and by imposing restrictions on the power of the church. He granted complete freedom of religion in 1781, abolished monasteries to make room for temporal responsibilities. Under his rule, many humanitarian institutions were estab-

lished (general hospital in 1784). A reform in 1783 abolished municipal autonomy. In the century since the Turkish siege, the territory of Vienna had grown tenfold, its population had reached 235,000, and fully 300 manufactories were counted by 1790.

In the first half of the 19th century, absolutist-feudal principles gave way to the new bourgeois liberal ideals. It was the time of the French Revolution of 1789 and its aftermath: of Emperor Francis II/I (Austrian Empire from 1804); Napoleon's expansionist claims (Vienna was occupied in 1804 and again in 1809); of the state bankruptcy in 1811; of a new and important role zestfully played by the city during the Congress of Vienna in 1814/15 after Napoleon's defeat; and of the Metternich regime (a rigid police state, leading up to the March revolution of 1848). The bourgeois culture of the introspective *Biedermeier* flourished in the works of composers Beethoven, Schubert, Strauss and Lanner, authors Grillparzer, Raimund and Nestroy, and painters Waldmüller and Alt.

The dawning industrial age and its technical progress (steam ships on the Danube in 1823, gas utility in 1828, railroad in 1837) failed to eliminate mass unemployment or solve the housing crisis. Political oppression led to the revolution of 1848 which saw the middle-class, labour and students stand united in their fight against absolutism and censor ship. Their revolt was suppressed by the army, and Francis Joseph I (Emperor as of 1848) began his reign as a neo-absolutist monarch.

From the mid 19th century, Vienna turned into a major capital, commencing its *Gründerzeit*, a period characterised by an

The Turkish siege of Vienna, 1683. Contemporary painting, Historisches Museum.

unprecedented building boom. In 1850, the city assimilated its 34 suburbs located within the Gürtel, incorporating them as its 2nd to 8th District. Vienna was now home to 431,000 people. In 1857, the Emperor resolved on levelling the fortifications that had been encircling and confining the inner city since the mid 16th century. In their stead and spreading across the glacis, the Ringstrasse and its buildings, designed by the most famous architects of the period, came into existence over the following decades, as an urban *Gesamtkunstwerk* in the Historicist style.

The law (Industrial Code of 1859) looked after the bourgeois interests of a capitalist system, and the right to vote for a town council granted to Vienna once again in 1861 established an influential and liberally minded upper middle class. A long-distance water pipeline built in 1873, river training works on the Danube in 1875, a central cemetery and the development of a gas and electricity supply system improved the infrastructure of a city that had doubled its populace since 1850, by absorbing its outer ring of suburbs. The building boom, with low-quality housing tenements mushrooming all over the place in the late 19th century, irrevocably changed the appearance of the city.

Otto Wagner's municipal design project won an award - his buildings in the Vienna Secession style have become landmarks. The culture of the *"Ringstrassenzeit"* and the *Fin de siècle* were typified and immortalised by physicians such as Billroth, Hyrtl, Skoda and, later, Freud; composers Bruckner, Brahms and Mahler; through operettas written by Strauss, Millöcker, Suppé and

Lehár; by painters Makart, Feuerbach, Klimt and Schiele; and by writers Hamerling, Saar, Hofmannsthal, Schnitzler and Kraus.

With the Christian Socialists holding sway in politics from 1895 onwards (Lueger), there occurred a fundamental change in economic policy. Gas and electricity utilities were given over to municipal administration, and the city became active in health care and social welfare services. Vienna now housed 1.87 million people, and its area of 273 sq km already reached across the Danube.

At the end of World War I (1914 to 1918) - Francis Joseph I had died in 1916, and Charles I was forced to abdicate - the Republic of Deutsch-Österreich was founded on November 12, 1918. It spelled the end not just for the reign of the Habsburgs which had spanned more than six centuries of history; Vienna, residence of the Empire, centre and focus of the Austro-Hungarian monarchy, became the new federal capital of a new republic that had shrunk to narrow confines.

The new order established in Central Europe after 1918 brought in its wake many economic and social problems, supplying the final momentum for (already latent) social change. The first general elections in 1919 resulted in a majority for the Social Democrats in the Vienna City Council. In 1922, Vienna was separated from Lower Austria, becoming a city and province of equal status with the other Austrian provinces.

"Red Vienna", governed from 1919 to today by a Social Democrat majority, with the exception of the period of fascism, until 1934 produced model achievements, especially in housing, education, social welfare

The French cannonade of Vienna, May 1809. Contemporary engraving, Historisches Museum.

Vienna at the time of the International Exhibition, 1873. View towards the Old Town. Historisches Museum.

and health care. By 1933, more than 63,000 housing units had been thrown up under a municipal building scheme. Leading personalities of the time were Mayors Reumann and Seitz, Counsellors Breitner and Tandler, and Glöckel, reformer of the school system.

Latent tensions between the Christian Socialists and Social Democrats, and the shock effect of the global economic crisis cumulated in 1927 in a political court ruling which led to demonstrations by the Social Democrats and street fighting that left hundreds dead, followed by the rapid radicalisation of political antagonisms. In combination with the government's battle against "Red Vienna", this resulted in constant face-offs between the paramilitary units run by the Social Democrats (Republikanischer Schutzbund) and the government (Heimwehr and Frontkämpfer) and, finally, in February 1934, degenerated into civil war.

In the following period of Austro-fascism (authoritarian corporative state under Chancellor Dollfuss), the Social Democrat party was banned, the Council and Diet of Vienna were dissolved, and the city lost its status as a province, to be ruled directly by the federal government and its political aims adapted to the ideas of the authoritarian state.

The Austro-fascist regime, which drew its support from the Catholic church, steadily lost ground to the National Socialists in a conflict that had started right in 1934, and was toppled in March 1938 when German troops occupied the country. Vienna became a *Reichsgau*, governed directly by Berlin. The absorption of communities in Lower Austria boosted its territory from 270 to more than

1,200 sq km, and its districts from 21 to 26. In World War II (1939 to 1945), heavy bombardment from 1943 and the conquest of Vienna by the Red Army in April 1945 produced severe destruction. Some 21 percent of the buildings (also Stephansdom and Staatsoper), were damaged or lost. In September 1945, Vienna was divided into four occupation sectors by the victorious Allies, and Theodor Körner, a Social Democrat, was named its mayor.

After the Austrian State Treaty was signed on May 15, 1955, the allied troops were withdrawn. Of the communities merged with Vienna in 1938, 80 were returned to Lower Austria in 1954, so that the federal capital was left with 23 districts, covering a territory of 415 sq km. A "reconstruction programme" was put in place to repair the damage wrought by the war. Upon its completion, the municipality concentrated on improving the technical infrastructure and developing a city suitable for its people and their political, social and cultural needs.

The openness found in Vienna today has its roots in the naturally developed understanding of a citizenry that once was living in the capital of an empire which united many peoples and nations under its spell. The change in the political and economic situation in Eastern Europe taking place late in the 20th century has invested Vienna with a new importance thanks to its traditional links and position "in the heart of Europe". Vienna, situated for almost half a century at the frontier between the opposing ideologies of East and West, envisages its new role as a promising prerequisite for a future in the middle of change.

Vienna 1993. The rebuilt Danube bed with Danube island, UNO City and Vienna International Center.

PAGE 21

PAGE 31

PAGE 43

PAGE 53

PAGE 63

PAGE 75

THE OLD TOWN

1 · Old-town houses and church: Maria am Gestade.

2 · Irisgasse, a view of historic Naglergasse.

3 · Old-town house in Domgasse, corner of Blutgasse towards Grünangergasse.

4 · Old-town houses in Schreyvogelgasse, "Dreimäderlhaus".

5 · Old-town houses in Kurrentgasse, near Judenplatz.

6 · Old-town houses in Himmelpfortgasse.

7 · Historic Griechengasse, near Fleischmarkt.

8 · Old-town houses in Blumenstockgasse and Ballgasse.

9 · Stock-im-Eisen-Platz, Haas-Haus and Stephansdom.

10 · Freyung, Austriabrunnen and Schottenkirche.

11 · Stephansplatz, looking towards Kärntner Strasse.

12 · Michaelerplatz, Michaelerkirche and Hofburg.

14

13 · View from the spire of the Stephansdom: Michaelertrakt of the Hofburg, Michaelerkirche and Parlament (from left to right).

14 · Rooftops from Griechengasse and Hafnersteig towards the Stephansdom.

15 · A view of the Stephansdom from Am Hof: armoury, Baroque burgher residence, Palais Collalto (from left to right).

16 · Kärntner Strasse pedestrian zone, looking towards Ringstrasse.

17 · Ring-Galerien shopping mall, Kärntner Ring.

18 · Haas-Haus shopping mall, Stephansplatz.

19 · View from Graben to Stock-im-Eisen-Platz.

20 · View from Graben to Kohlmarkt and Michaelerplatz, Michaelertor at the Hofburg.

21 · View from Kohlmarkt (near Graben) towards the Stephansdom.

22 · View of the Volksgarten towards the Stephansdom.

23 · View across Franz-Josefs-Kai towards the Stephansdom.

24 · View across the Burgtheater towards the Stephansdom.

THE EMPERORS' HOUSE

1 · Volksgarten and fountain, looking towards Ringstrasse.

2 · Burggarten, exhibition conservatory and greenhouse.

3 · Volksgarten, rose garden, view of the Burgtheater.

4 · View from Ringstrasse to Heldenplatz, monument to Archduke Charles.

5 · Volksgarten. Monument to Empress Elisabeth, with the Burgtheater in the background.

6 · Ringstrasse, Volksgarten, Heldenplatz and Neue Burg. Foreground (from left to right): Theseustempel, monuments to Prince Eugene and Archduke Charles.
24

res Burgtor (with the Kunsthistorisches Museum to the right). Background (centre): Schloss Belvedere and Karlskirche.

7 · Hofburg, Winterreitschule. Spanish Riding School.

8 · Josefsplatz, monument to Joseph II, Nationalbibliothek.

9 · Hofburg, stables, Renaissance courtyard.

10 · Neue Burg, stairs at Heldenplatz.

11 · Hofburg, grand library hall (Nationalbibliothek). Domed hall and northern wing.

12 · Hofburg, Amalienburg. Imperial banquet table (dining hall).

13 · Hofburg, Schweizerhof. Treasure house, imperial crown.

14 · Hofburg, Amalienburg. Alexander-Appartements.

15 · Hofburg, Amalienburg. Elisabeth-Appartements.

28

16 · Hofburg, Leopoldinischer Trakt. Maria-Theresien-Appartement, mirror hall.

17 · Burggarten. Statue of Emperor Francis Joseph I.

18 · Neue Burg. Monuments to Prince Eugene and Archduke Charles.

19 · Platz In der Burg, monument to Emperor Francis I, Schweizertor.

20 · Kapuzinergruft, Kaisergruft, tomb of the Habsburgs.

30

GOD'S HOUSES

1 · Votivkirche. Crossing vault, decorative painting.

2 · Peterskirche. Dome, Baroque dome fresco.

3 · Universitätskirche (church of the Jesuits). Nave vault.

4 · Luegerkirche (Zentralfriedhof). *Jugendstil* dome ornaments.

5 · Karlskirche. Dome, Baroque dome fresco.

6 · Altlerchenfelder Kirche. Crossing-dome, decorative painting.

7 · Fünfhauser Kirche (Maria vom Siege). Decorated dome.

8 · Dominikanerkirche. Dome and vault of the nave.

9 · Piaristenkirche. Plague column dedicated to Mary on Jodok-Fink-Platz.

10 · Dreifaltigkeitskirche. Courtyard of the Allgemeines Krankenhaus.

11 · Ulrichskirche, Ulrichsplatz, view from Neustiftgasse.

12 · Salesianerinnenkirche. Door in the portal leading to the forecourt.

13 · Kirche Am Hof (Alte Jesuitenkirche). Platz am Hof and Mariensäule.

14 · Kirche Am Steinhof. Church of the Vienna Psychiatric Hospital.

15 · Karlskirche. View from Karlsplatz.

16 · Michaelerkiche. Choir, stucco relief "Fall of the Angels".

17 · Greek (non-uniate) Church, Fleischmarkt. Nave.

18 · Synagogue in Seitenstettengasse, domed hall.

19 · Servitenkirche, ovoid domed hall.

20 · Stephansdom, northern side. Unfinished northern spire and belfry (left), Romanesque western façade (right). Stephansplatz.

21 · Stephansdom. View of the vault. Clustered pier and diamond vault of the three-nave main building.

22 · Stephansdom. Romanesque western portal with figural ornaments.

23 · Stephansdom. Gothic organ base, statue of St. Sebastian.

24 · Universitätskirche (Jesuitenkirche), Baroque pulpit.

25 · Kirche Am Steinhof, *Jugendstil* portal crowning element.

A RING OF SPLENDOUR AND OPULENCE

1 · Staatsoper, stairs to the Ringstrasse.

2 · Burgtheater. Ceiling picture, grand northern staircase.

3 · Kunsthistorisches Museum, staircase.

4 · Justizpalast, central hall with grand flight of stairs.

44

5 · Akademie der bildenden Künste, ceiling of the central hall.

6 · Museum für angewandte Kunst, staircase.

7 · Rathaus, stairs to grand hall (Feststiege I).

8 · Burgtheater, staircase (grand southern staircase).

9 · Akademie der bildenden Künste. Monument to Schiller.

10 · Kriegsministerium (Regierungsgebäude), façade facing Ringstrasse.

11 · Postsparkasse, central projection. Monument to Georg Coch.

12 · Parlament, central entrance hall.

46

13 · Grand hall of the Musikvereinsgebäude, New Year's Concert.

47

14 · View across Maria-Theresien-Platz and the monument to Maria Theresa towards the Kunsthistorisches Museum.

15 · View across Stadtpark, Wien River and the vaulting thrown across the Wien River towards Karlskirche.

16 · Kunsthistorisches Museum, gallery of paintings.

17 · Parlament, portico of columns. View towards Ringstrasse.

18 · Naturhistorisches Museum, showroom.

19 · Rathaus, fronting square and Christmas market.

20 · Ringstrasse between Volksgarten and Rathauspark (from left to right): Parlament, Rathaus, Votivkirche and Universität.

21 · Donaukanal. Part of the former Kaiserbad lock.

22 · Wien River near the Donaukanal, pedestrians' and underground bridges.

23 · Mouth of the Wien River at the Donaukanal. Urania observatory.

24 · Wien River portal. Vaulting at Stadtpark.

WITNESSES OF POWER AND GLORY

1 · Unteres Belvedere, marble hall. Fountain by Donner.

2 · Unteres Belvedere, mirror hall. sculpture of Prince Eugene.

3 · Palais Schwarzenberg, marble gallery.

4 · Prince Eugene's winter palais, staircase.

54

5 · View from Rennweg across Unteres Belvedere and the park to Oberes Belvedere.

6 · Schönbrunn, garden side. View across the grand parterre of the palace grounds.

7 · Schönbrunn, rooms open to the public. "Millionen-Zimmer".

8 · Schönbrunn, rooms open to the public. Grand gallery (grand hall).

9 · Schönbrunn, ceremonial hall.

10 · Schönbrunn, the garden suite.

11 · Palais Kinsky, staircase.

12 · Garden palais Liechtenstein, marble hall. Ceiling fresco.

13 · Palais Lobkowitz, staircase.

14 · City palais Liechtenstein, staircase.

15 · Aula of the Alte Universität, grand hall. Ceiling fresco.

16 · Palais Pallavicini (Palais Fries), grand hall.

17 · Theresianum (Old Favorita), Maria-Theresien-Appartement.

18 · Schloss Hetzendorf, garden hall.

19 · Albertina (Palais Taroucca), staircase.

20 · Hermesvilla, Empress Elisabeth's bedroom.

WAITING TO BE SEEN AND LOVED

1 · Baroque burgher house, Sonnenfelsgasse.

2 · Baroque burgher house, portal crowning element. Schwertgasse.

3 · Baroque burgher house, Ulrichsplatz.

4 · Old-town lane, former suburb, Spittelberg.

5 · Burgher house in the Classic Revival style, Annagasse.

6 · *Sezession*-style commercial building. Loos-Haus, Michaelerplatz.

7 · *Jugendstil* residential block, Rechte Wienzeile.

8 · Strudelhofstiege, a staircase off Liechtensteinstrasse.

9 · Municipal housing project, "Hundertwasserhaus". Löwengasse.

10 · Kärntner Strasse pedestrian zone, café.

11 · Street market in Kutschkergasse.

12 · Stephansplatz pedestrian zone, towards Graben.

13 · "Karl-Marx-Hof" housing project, central block. Typical pioneering municipal housing in the First Republic.

14 · Concert of the "Musikalischer Sommer". Schönbrunn.

15 · Vienna Boys Choir, park of Augarten Palais.

16 · Touring company of the District Festival Weeks. Amerlinghaus.

17 · Concert of the Vienna Festival Weeks. Grand Hall at the Konzerthaus.

18 · Opera Ball, Staatsoper. Dance floor made up by connecting the stalls and stage.

19 · Garden of the restaurant *Zur Goldenen Glocke*. Schönbrunner Strasse.

20 · District party of the Vienna Festival Weeks. Schlosserplatz.

21 · Coffee-house. Cafe Sperl, Gumpendorfer Strasse.

22 · *Heuriger* wine tavern. Pfarrplatz, Heiligenstadt.

23 · Wurstelprater amusement park. View of the giant Ferriswheel with the old city and Stephansdom in the background.

24 · View from Leopoldsberg to the Danube, Danube Island and New Danube. From left to right: Old Danube (far left), Danube Tower, UNO City and bridges

(In front to back): Nordbrücke, Floridsdorferbrücke, Nordbahnbrücke, Brigittenauerbrücke, Reichsbrücke, Praterbrücke and Ostbahnbrücke.

25 · View across Wildgrube to Leopoldsberg.

26 · Lobau recreational area. Dead Danube channel. Alte Naufahrt.

27 · Prater. Walk near Lusthaus.

28 · Lower Old Danube, near the Gänsehäufl beach.

The text printed in bold
above the notes indicates
the title and page numbers of the relevant part
of the picture section, followed by the numbers
of the photos commented.
The text summarises groups of photos or related
single photos as subjects.
Only major subjects are discussed,
and not all photos are commented.

The city of Vienna is geographically located
on 16° 22' 27" east longitude of Greenwich
and 48° 12' 32" northern latitude,
with the Stephansdom spire as reference point.
The city terrace is situated 170 metres above sea level;
reaching the highest altitude on Hermannskogel
at 542 metres, and the lowest altitude
in the Lobau forest at 151 metres.
In 1992, the highest and lowest temperatures were 36.4°C
and -10.0°C respectively.
Vienna's climate is in a transition zone
where the cool, rainy summers and
mild winters of the maritime climate
alternate with the hot, dry summers and cold winters
of the continental climate.
Vienna covers a territory of 414.95 square kilometres,
or 0.5% of the territory of Austria.
Its population numbers 1,539,848,
or 20% of the Austrian population
and 24% of the country's workforce.
The territory is broken down in 23 districts:
I. Innere Stadt, II. Leopoldstadt,
III. Landstrasse, IV. Wieden, V. Margareten,
VI. Mariahilf, VII Neubau, VIII. Josefstadt,
IX. Alsergrund, X. Favoriten, XI. Simmering,
XII. Meidling, XIII. Hietzing, XIV. Penzing,
XV. Rudolfsheim-Fünfhaus, XVI. Ottakring,
XVII. Hernals, XVIII. Währing,
XIX. Döbling, XX. Brigittenau,
XXI. Floridsdorf, XXII. Donaustadt,
and XXIII. Liesing.

The Old Town from the south: Stadtpark, houses fronting the Ringstrasse and Stephansdom.

The Old Town from the north: Peterskirche (dome), Michaelerkirche and dome.

View across Rathauspark, Ringstrasse, Volksgarten and Heldenplatz towards the Neue Burg.

THE OLD TOWN
Pages 11 to 20
Photos 1 · 2 · 3 · 5 · 7 · 8 · 14

The oldest quarters. Medieval Vienna, rising partly above the ruins and debris of an ancient Roman camp in the first half of the second millenium and since become the district of Innere Stadt, has left its traces in countless streets, squares and houses of the old town. Greatly altered in their external appearance by the passage of centuries of ever changing building fashions, they are still pervaded by an aura of ancient history. **Am Gestade** and **Griechengasse**. Around the church of Maria am Gestade (first mentioned in 1158) and in the narrow lane of Griechengasse, historic houses are still standing where they were once built on a bluff overlooking a navigable branch of the Danube. The precipice had already served to protect parts of the Roman fortress. Along Griechengasse/Hafnersteig, a Gothic fortress-house tower has survived which was once part of the medieval fortifications. The row of houses in Naglergasse, westward of Irisgasse, with its basically late Gothic buildings provides an impressive reminiscence of the old town of Vienna. The lane follows the wall of the Roman camp, and some of its houses are built on stones left over from the wall. The neighbourhood of **Domgasse** and **Blutgasse** is among the oldest and most interesting parts of the old town (dating back to the 14th century). The historically valuable ensembles, with their romantic inner courts, have been ideally refurbished in modern times.
Blumenstockgasse, **Ballgasse** and **Kurrentgasse** have houses that still breathe the flavour of the Middle Ages, their medieval substance recognisable in spite of the contrasting styles of their façades.

Photos 10 · 12 · 15 · 19 · 20

Historical streets and squares. In the inner city, the medieval network of streets and squares has been preserved in its historical arrangement. **Am Hof**, a square named after the Babenberg court built here in 1155, and still bordered by valuable historical buildings, was used as a market place, which enjoyed its greatest popularity in the 19th century when it was the site of the Christmas market. Until the demolition of some houses in the mid 19th century, nothing but a narrow lane linked the square to the **Freyung** and the Schottenstift, an abbey founded by the Babenbergs in 1155. The Freyung, again surrounded by a noteworthy assembly of old houses, once was the place of execution, a Baroque place for merriment, fairground for stalls, wandering performers and jugglers, and Christmas market for 70 years after 1772. **Michaelerplatz** has its origins in a suburban village that had sprung up at the intersection of two Roman roads. Nearby, the first Burg, castle and residence of the rulers, was built in the 13th century. Apart from Michaelerkirche, a church, and the Grosses Michaelerhaus, most of the built-up space came into existence in the late 19th (Michaelertrakt of the Hofburg) and early 20th century (Loos-Haus, in the Secession style). The **Kohlmarkt** leads to the **Graben**, which was once a moat running along the early medieval wall and was filled in to make room for new houses. Both were important market places from the 13th century. The Graben, venue of court festivities in the 17th and 18th century, and the Kohlmarkt today are among the most distinguished shopping streets of Vienna and major promenades of urban life (pedestrian zone).

THE EMPEROR'S HOUSE
Pages 21 to 30
Photos 2 · 6 · 7-12 · 14 · 18 · 19

Hofburg. Projects to harmonise the mixed-style collection of residential court buildings called Hofburg, advanced in the late Baroque period and again in the 19th century ("Kaiserforum" – a forum worthy of emperors) never quite materialised. Noticeable periods in the development of the complex are indicated by Gothic elements in the Schweizerhof, early Baroque buildings at the square In der Burg, late Baroque structures along Josefsplatz, and Historicist architecture on Heldenplatz. The **Schweizerhof**, oldest part of the Hofburg (Gothic chapel), replaced the first castle which had been begun in 1275. Following extensions around 1450, the **Stallburg** as well as the **Amalienburg**, originally detached Renaissance buildings, were added a century later. The latter was connected to the Schweizerhof in the second half of the 17th century by a wing named **Leopoldinischer Trakt**. Major projects in the Baroque period included the library building of the **Hofbibliothek** on Josefsplatz, the **Reichskanzleitrakt**, an administrative building which connects the Schweizerhof to the Amalienburg (creating the enclosure In der Burg), the **Winterreitschule**, linking up the stables in the Stallburg, and the **Redoutensäle**, ballrooms for festive occasions. In the early 19th century, gardens (**Burggarten** and **Volksgarten**) and the **Äusseres Burgtor** were built on the bastions. When the fortifications were razed in the 1850s, the **Neue Burg** and two museums were built as the last extension of the Hofburg, in line with the "Kaiserforum" design.
The **Michaelertrakt** completed the front of the Hofburg towards the inner city at the end of the 19th century.

Ruprechtskirche. The oldest church of Vienna, built in the 11th (9th?) century on a former cliff.

The lanes of the Ringstrasse near the Stadtpark, towards Schwarzenbergplatz. Karlskirche.

Palais Trautson (former suburb of St. Ulrich). Magnificent Baroque building, 1712.

GOD'S HOUSES
Pages 31 to 42
Photos 2 · 3 · 5 · 8 · 13 - 15 · 19 · 20 · 25

The **Ruprechtskirche** in the oldest part of Vienna was the original parish church. The first building of the **Stephansdom**, erected in the Romanesque style outside the town wall, was completed in 1160 and became the new parish church. The Babenbergs, rulers of the town from 1135 onwards, had invested the Bishop of Passau with the churches of Vienna (Treaty of Mautern, 1137). The second church, in the Late Romanesque style, was dedicated in 1263. Of this building, the western façade with the Riesentor and the two Heidentürme have survived. Today's Gothic cathedral is the third church, built between 1304 and 1525: the hall-choir in 1340, the southern tower in 1433, and the nave in 1440. Building at the northern tower was stopped in 1523 (belfry in 1578). St. Stephan has a host of unique works of art inside and at its outer walls, crypts below the choir and catacombs dug in the early 18th century for burial. The cathedral, extensively damaged in 1945 and repaired by 1952, ranks among Europe's most famous churches. It is Austria's greatest Gothic building and a landmark of Vienna. Its spire rises 136.7 m. **Kirche am Hof**, **Jesuitenkirche**, **Dominikanerkirche** and **Servitenkirche** are early Baroque churches that celebrated the successful Counter-Reformation in the early 17th century by numerous foundations of monasteries which left their indelible mark on the cityscape. **Peterskirche** and **Karlskirche** are high Baroque churches erected in 1733 and 1739 respectively. The Karlskirche symbolises the universal imperial claim of its founder, Charles VI. The church **Am Steinhof** is a *Jugendstil-Gesamtkunstwerk* created in the early 20th century.

A RING OF SPLENDOUR AND OPULENCE
Pages 43 to 52
Photos 1 - 9 · 12 - 14 · 16 - 20

The **Ringstrasse** boulevard was built in the second half of the 19th century in the place of the former fortifications. Shaped like a polygonal, it almost completely encircles the old town except along the Donaukanal. Detailed plans provided for the boulevard and adjacent area to be lined by the major public buildings; similarly, the aristocracy and liberal upper middle class sought to express themselves in magnificent houses and palaces. The most famous architects and master artists of the period strove to produce a *Gesamtkunstwerk* — the ensemble of the Ringstrasse, its buildings and its interieurs became world-famous as typifying the style of Historicism. The main buildings along or near the Ringstrasse are: **Staatsoper**, completed as the court opera house in 1869, the first Historicist building along the Ringstrasse which holds one of Europe's largest stages; **Burgtheater**, built as the court theatre in 1888 in the Italian Renaissance style with resplendent grand staircases in its wings; **Parlament**, housing the two legislative chambers and erected in 1883 in the Greek style; **Rathaus**, a monumental neo-Gothic town hall with splendid staircases, grand hall and meeting room for the town council, finished in 1885; **Votivkirche**, a neo-Gothic memorial church from 1879; the two **Museums**, which made up part of the Kaiserforum, their shells, Italian Renaissance, finished in 1881; **Musikvereinsgebäude** (1869) for concert performances, **Museum für angewandte Kunst** (Museum of Applied Art) in 1871; **Akademie der bildenden Künste** (Academy of Fine Arts) in 1876; **Börse** (Exchange) in 1877; **Justizpalast** (Hall of Justice) in 1881; and many more.

WITNESSES OF POWER AND GLORY
Pages 53 to 62
Photos 1 · 2 · 5 · 6 - 10

After its decisive victory over the Turks, the Baroque "imperial capital and residential town" in the early 18th century experienced the greatest and most sweeping architectural, artistic and cultural change in its history. Suburban villages sprouted palaces, summer seats and mansions for the nobility and middle class. The period's most resplendent palaces are Schönbrunn, imperial château de plaisance, and Belvedere, residence of Prince Eugene of Savoy. **Schönbrunn**, replacing a castle destroyed by the Turks in 1683, was begun based on a design by J.B. Fischer v. Erlach in 1696, for Joseph I and, after conversions, completed in its current design by Nikolaus Pacassi for Maria Theresa in 1749. Its sumptuous interieur was designed by Pacassi in the Rococo style. A large park was laid out in 1706, and remodelled in the French mode in 1765. It held the garden parterre, Neptune's fountain, a Roman ruin, waterfall and obelisk, the Schöner Brunnen (pavilion guarding the well that gave the palace its name), the circular-shaped zoo, Gloriette and, in 1882, the botanical gardens and glasshouse. The **Belvedere** was erected for Prince Eugene by Lukas v. Hildebrandt in 1723 as a summer residence with two palaces and a sloping terraced park inbetween. The upper wing was used for social events, the lower wing served residential purposes. The Belvedere, positioned to enjoy a splendid view over Vienna, and its lavish interieur competed with the splendour of the court projects, but on Prince Eugene's death was acquired by the emperor with all its works of art. Schönbrunn and Belvedere rank among Europe's most handsome and exquisite palaces.

Palais Neupauer-Breuner, portal, 1716. Baroque palace designed for several families.

A *Durchhaus*: a public thoroughway between two streets that cuts across backyards and wings.

Naschmarkt. Year-round market, held on top of the vault across the Wien River.

Photos 3 · 4 · 11 · 12 · 14 · 16 · 18 - 20
Examples of **palaces** built between the early 18th and late 19th century: **Palais Schwarzenberg**, begun in 1697 (J. L. v. Hildebrandt), remodelled and completed in 1728 by J. E. Fischer v. Erlach), early Baroque garden palais, a riding school and orangerie added in 1751, noteworthy: marble gallery; Prince Eugene's **Winterpalais**, a Baroque town palace built by J. L. v. Hildebrandt and J. B. Fischer v. Erlach in 1696 to 1724, one of the most charming Baroque buildings of Vienna, noteworthy: façade, staircases and grand apartments; **Stadtpalais Liechtenstein**, a Baroque building erected in 1694 to 1705 by Gabriele de Gabrielis, with interieur dating from 1840 (Second Rococo), noteworthy: staircase; **Gartenpalais Liechtenstein** (Rossau), built in the Baroque style by D. Martinelli in 1711, noteworthy: Sala terrena (passageway), grand staircases and marble hall; **Palais Kinsky**, Baroque town palace made by J. L. v. Hildebrandt for Count Daun in 1717, de-volved to the Kinskys in 1784, noteworthy: façade and staircase; **Schloss Hetzendorf**, Baroque country seat converted by J. L. v. Hildebrandt in 1712, extended for Maria Theresa by N. Pacassi in 1743, noteworthy: reception hall; **Palais Pallavicini** (frieze), Classicist town seat built by J. F. Hetzendorf v. Hohenberg in 1784, noteworthy: interieur; **Albertina**, build in the 1750s, expanded in 1804 and remodelled along Classicist lines in the mid 1850s, noteworthy: staircase, main hall (Kornhäusl); **Hermesvilla**, built by Karl Hasenauer for Empress Elisabeth in 1886 as a historical country villa, noteworthy: decora-tive painting (Makart).

WAITING TO BE SEEN AND LOVED
Pages 63 to 74
Photos 1 - 9 · 11 · 12 · 13 · 16 · 24
Ordinary exteriors in Vienna. With their ornate façades, splendid entrances and inner courts full of greenery, the houses built in the Baroque period by the upper middle class after 1683 were scale-models of the palaces erected by the nobility. The houses of tradesfolk and government officials, built on small lots, were simpler in their arrangement, with the storeys accessed across "Pawlatschen", balcony-type passageways. Next to them, houses for the poor were built as uniform, multi-level tenement houses, to be replaced, in the age of industrialisation, by a new type of estate housing, used to fill in building sites in line with a general regulation scheme that left little room to design individu-ality. Baroque and Biedermeier domiciles for the bourgeois, the boom-driven designs of the Gründerzeit, residential blocks in the Vienna Secession style, housing projects for the poor thrown up between the two world wars that were pioneering in their concept, and the singular buildings of modern architects make a cityscape that is unique to observe. This special assembly of architectural characters, acquired by centuries of living, made up by opposites such as Loos-Haus, Hundert-wasser-Haus, Otto Wagner's houses, Karl-Marx-Hof, Spittelberg, Strudelhofstiege, green Biedermeier courts, passages and Haas-Haus, smiles at us through a web of crow's-feet, showing us a city grown through and cultivated by its people. Careful attention to historical detail and the creation and development of new residential and recrea-tional areas for urban social life (Donauinsel) have produced salient achievements for modern Vienna.

Photos 10 · 11 · 19 · 21 - 28
The Viennese way of life has generated several unique institutions that offer an in-depth experience of and insight into the populace. The Vienna **Kaffeehaus** is known to the world for its waiters, called "Herr Ober", the high art of coffee making and drinking, desserts such as the Apfelstrudel, and generations of literary luminates and other celebrities that passed through and stayed on. The **Beisel** is a small place that preserves the tradition of inexpensive and sound local food. The **Heuriger** (the name for the new wine and the tavern that serves it) can be found in profu-sion in the north-western suburbs: they all offer skin-deep contact with the city's culture and local flavour. The **Naschmarkt** and many other street markets that supply urbanites with fruits, vegetables and other needs contribute a special nuance to the local colour. Within its territory, Vienna offers a great variety of recreational spaces. The **Wienerwald**, a forest and airlung, spreads across undulating hills to the west, in contrast to the wetlands of the **Prater** (opened to the public in 1766) and **Obere Lobau**, formerly reserved to imperial shooting parties, which harbour the last remains of primeval river forests. The Volksprater, the forest adjoining the city, was given over to entertainment after 1766. River training works in 1875 separated the old main branch of the Danube from its new course, thereby creating the **Alte Donau**, a paradise for swimming and relaxing. Further training works in 1972 produced the **Donauinsel**, a river island, and a second Danube arm, both giant new recreational areas in the immediate vicinity of the city.

Additional notes.

Dust jacket
Details of façades of *Jugendstil* residential buildings designed by Otto Wagner, Linke Wienzeile 38 (front), Linke Wienzeile 40 (back).

Endpapers
Left: detail of Ringstrasse next to Parlament, "Rossebändiger", Athene-Brunnen and Rathaus tower.
Right: Johann Strauss monument, Stadtpark

Half-title
View from Parlament: Stephansdom, Michaelerkirche and Michaelerkuppel of the Burg.

Full title
Left: View from Stock-im-Eisen-Platz across Graben to Kohlmarkt.
Right: Biedermeier dress, Vienna Fashion Collection: flag at the Federal President's seat, Hofburg; Baroque house, detailed façade of Hochholzerhof; street musician, Michaelerplatz; carnival parade, Ringstrasse near Oper; memorial against war and fascism, Albertinaplatz; Mozart's grave, St. Marxer Friedhof; Johann Strauss monument, Stadtpark.

Intermediate titles
Page 5
Mautern Treaty of Exchange, 1137. First mention of Vienna as a *civitas*, Bayerisches Hauptstaatsarchiv, Munich.
Page 11
Palais Obizzi, Vienna Clock Museum.
Page 21
Prince Eugene's equestrian statue and central projection of Neue Burg, Heldenplatz.
Page 31
Schutzmantelmadonna. Gothic statue on a pillar in Stephansdom.
Page 43
Statue of Viktoria on the Liebenberg monument (Dr.-Karl-Lueger-Ring), Rathaus tower and statue.
Page 53
View across the pond towards Oberes Belvedere.
Page 63
Jugendstil residential buildings, Linke Wienzeile 38 and 40, partial view.
Page 75
Inn sign, listing the menu.

All statistical data quoted herein are from the Statistisches Jahrbuch der Stadt Wien and from the Austrian Central Statistical Office. All data compiled on the basis of material valid by the end of 1993.

Also by the author:

Published by Jugend & Volk Verlag:

Ernst Hausner
Wien
308 pages, 865 colour pictures, 1988.
Text in German, English and Italian.

Ernst Hausner
Vienna,
Strolling Through a Beautiful City
120 pages, 444 colour pictures, 1993.
This book has also been published in German, French and Italian.

Ernst Hausner
Vienna,
Strolling Trough an Unknown City
120 pages, 363 colour pictures, also published in german, 1994.

Ernst Hausner
Österreich
252 pages, 842 colour pictures, 1986.
Text in German, English and Italian.

Ernst Hausner
Niederösterreich
206 pages, 743 colour pictures, 1989.

Published by Edition Hausner:

Ernst Hausner
Burgenland
172 pages, 536 colour pictures, 1990.

Ernst Hausner
Styria
Published in English,
212 pages, 880 colour pictures, 1992.

Ernst Hausner
Oberösterreich
206 pages, 753 colour pictures, 1995.

Ernst Hausner
Austria
100 pages, 315 colour pictures,
also published in Chinese, French, German, Italian, Japanese and Russian, 1996.